Jackie Robinson
Plays Ball

Jackie Robinson

Plays Ball

By Robyn O'Sullivan

NATIONAL GEOGRAPHIC

Washington, D.C.

Founded in 1888, the National Geographic Society is one of the largest nonprofit scientific and educational organizations in the world. It reaches more than 285 million people worldwide each month through its official journal, NATIONAL GEOGRAPHIC, and its four other magazines; the National Geographic Channel; television documentaries; radio programs; films; books; videos and DVDs; maps; and interactive media. National Geographic has funded more than 8,000 scientific research projects and supports an education program combating geographic illiteracy.

For more information, please call
1-800-NGS-LINE (647-5463) or write to the following address:

National Geographic Society
1145 17th Street N.W.
Washington, D.C. 20036-4688
U.S.A.

Visit us online at www.nationalgeographic.com/books

For information about special discounts for bulk purchases, please contact
National Geographic Books Special Sales at ngspecsales@ngs.org

For rights or permissions inquiries, please contact National Geographic
Books Subsidiary Rights: ngbookrights@ngs.org

Library of Congress Cataloging-in-Publication Data

O'Sullivan, Robyn.
  Jackie Robinson plays ball / by Robyn O'Sullivan.
    p. cm. – (National Geographic history chapters)
  ISBN 978-1-4263-0190-2 (library)
1. Robinson, Jackie, 1919-1972–Juvenile literature.   2. Baseball players–United States–Biography–Juvenile literature.   3. African American baseball players–Biography–Juvenile literature.   4. Brooklyn Dodgers (Baseball team)–History–Juvenile literature.   I. Title.
GV865.R6O39 2007
796.357092–dc22
[B]

2007007893

Photo Credits
Front Cover, 2-3, 8, 10, 11, 12, 14, 15, 16, 18, 19, 20, 22-23, 25, 26, 30, 31: © Bettmann/CORBIS; Spine, Endpage: © Shutterstock; 6, 27: © Time Life Pictures/Getty Images; 13: © Photodisc; 24: © Diamond Images/Getty Images; 28: © Ted Streshinsky/CORBIS; 32: © Mario Tama/Getty Images; 34, 35: © Nam Y. Huh/Associated Press.

Contents

Brooklyn Dodgers' Jackie Robinson stops short after rounding third base in the third game of the 1955 World Series against the Yankees.

Meet Jackie Robinson

Jackie Robinson is famous because he was a great baseball player. He is also famous because he was the first African American to play professional baseball in the major leagues.

In 1947, Robinson joined the Brooklyn Dodgers. At that time, African-American people were segregated, or kept separate, from whites. They had separate schools, restaurants, parks, and theaters. They also had separate sports teams. Jackie Robinson helped change that.

At the University of California at Los Angeles (UCLA), Jackie Robinson won the national championship in the long jump.

Chapter 1

The Early Years

Jack Roosevelt Robinson was born in Georgia in 1919. His father was a poor farmer. Before Jackie was one year old, his parents separated. He moved to Pasadena, California, with his mother, sister, and three brothers. They were the only African Americans in their neighborhood.

While he was growing up, Jackie's mother taught him about self-respect. She encouraged him to be confident and to use his talents. At school and college, Robinson was very good at sports. He was on the basketball, football, baseball, and track teams.

At UCLA, Robinson was an All-American halfback.

Robinson was an excellent runner and jumper. His teammates admired his athletic skills. He was popular with the other players.

In 1941, Robinson left college and went to Hawaii to play football with the Honolulu Bears. It was not a segregated team. Both African-American and white players played for the Bears. Robinson worked for a construction company in Hawaii and played football on weekends.

Jackie Robinson served as an officer during World War II.

At that time, many countries around the world were at war. On December 7, 1941, Japanese airplanes attacked Pearl Harbor in Hawaii. After that, America was at war, too. Robinson joined the United States Army and became one of the first African Americans to train as an army officer. He became a second lieutenant at a time when almost all officers were white.

After leaving the army, Robinson joined a baseball team in the Negro American League. He was playing shortstop for the Kansas City Monarchs when a man named Branch Rickey saw him play.

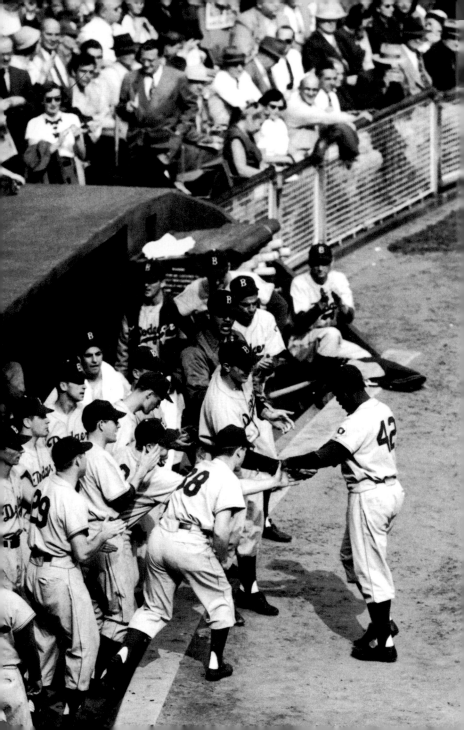

Chapter 2

Robinson Joins the Dodgers

Branch Rickey loved baseball. He had worked as a player, a coach, and a manager. The only thing Rickey didn't like about baseball was segregation. He thought it was unfair that African Americans weren't allowed to play baseball in the major leagues. Rickey decided to do something about it when he became the manager of the Brooklyn Dodgers.

◀ Robinson's home runs helped his teammates welcome him as a fellow athlete.

In the segregated South, train and bus stations had separate waiting rooms for African-Americans.

Rickey looked for an African-American baseball player to join the Brooklyn Dodgers. He was worried that the first African American to play major league baseball would be called names and treated badly by some people. Rickey knew he would have to find a special man for the job.

In 1945, Branch Rickey met Jackie
Robinson. He had seen Robinson play and
knew he was a great baseball player. Rickey
talked to Robinson and realized he was
easygoing and patient. Rickey knew he had
found the right man to help end racial
segregation in baseball.

**Branch Rickey persuaded Robinson to leave the Kansas City
Monarchs and sign a contract to join the Brooklyn Dodgers.**

Robinson hit a home run in his first game, with the Montreal Royals.

On October 23, 1945, Branch Rickey made a historic announcement. Jackie Robinson, an African-American baseball player, had signed a contract with the Brooklyn Dodgers. For the first year, Robinson would play for the Dodgers' minor-league team, the Montreal Royals.

In 1946, Robinson married Rachel Isum. They had met at UCLA, where she was a nursing student. Jackie and Rachel went to spring training in Florida. This was not an easy time for Robinson. Some teams refused to play even practice games against a team with an African-American player.

Finally, it was time for the first game of the season. Robinson played second base. He was very nervous, but he knew he had to keep his mind on the game. He hit a home run over the left field fence when he came up to bat in the third inning. The crowd went wild.

Robinson's first game was a success. He played well throughout the season. His batting average led the league. The Montreal Royals won the minor-league championship that year.

Robinson catches a fly ball.

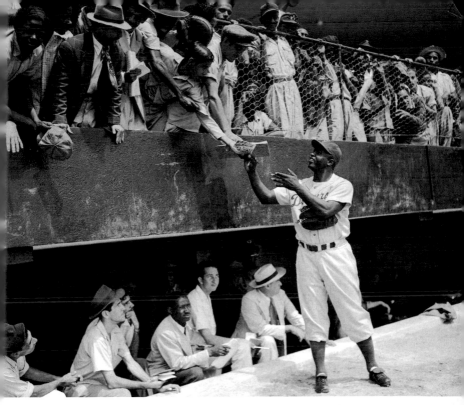

Although many in the crowd didn't cheer for Robinson, he did have his fans.

The next year, Robinson began to play with the Brooklyn Dodgers. On April 15, 1947, the rookie played his first game as a Dodger. He played first base, a position he had never played, but he learned quickly. Robinson's amazing career as a major-league baseball player had begun.

In 1949, Jackie Robinson received the Baseball Writers Most Valuable Player (MVP) Award.

Chapter 3

An All-Star Career

All through his first season with the Dodgers, Robinson was one of the best players in the major leagues. The Brooklyn Dodgers won the National League championship that year, Robinson hit 12 home runs and was named Rookie of the Year for 1947. This is the award for the best new player.

During the 1949 season, Robinson had the highest batting average (.342) in the league. He also led the league in stolen bases. Sportswriters named him the National League's Most Valuable Player (MVP).

Robinson was a great all-around player. He could hit, field, and steal bases. However, the crowds didn't always cheer him. Sometimes people called him mean, ugly names or spat at him. Robinson even received letters from people who threatened to kill him if he kept playing with "a white team."

It wasn't only the crowds at ball games that made life hard for Robinson. During some games, players on other teams threw the ball straight at his head. Other players yelled at him when he was at bat.

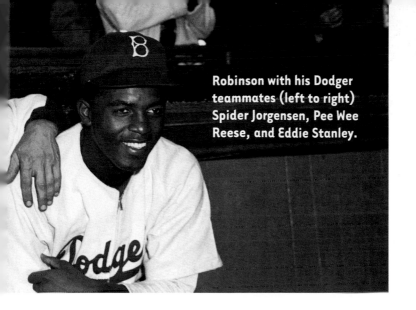

Robinson with his Dodger teammates (left to right) Spider Jorgensen, Pee Wee Reese, and Eddie Stanley.

Robinson had problems with segregation away from the playing field, too. When the Dodgers were traveling in the South, Jackie wasn't allowed to eat in the same restaurants or stay in the same hotels as his teammates. If Robinson had broken these segregation laws, he would have been sent to jail.

Robinson was friends with some of his teammates. They helped him to ignore the insults and bad treatment and not fight back. He knew the best thing to do was just to play good baseball.

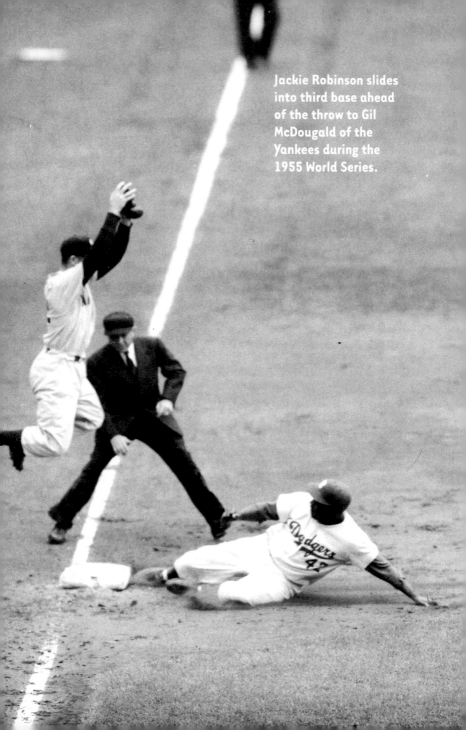

Jackie Robinson slides into third base ahead of the throw to Gil McDougald of the Yankees during the 1955 World Series.

Robinson played for the Brooklyn Dodgers for ten years. During that time, he often had the team's best batting average and stole the most bases. While he was with the Dodgers, they won the National League championship six times. In 1955, they won the World Series. A year later, Robinson announced his retirement as a professional baseball player.

Rachel Robinson and Jackie Jr. watch as newly retired Jackie Robinson hangs up his baseball glove in the trophy room of their family home.

Jackie Robinson's wife Rachel and his youngest son David admire the award he received for his efforts to end segregation.

Robinson became one of baseball's all-time greatest players. He won several baseball awards. Robinson also received awards for helping put an end to segregation. Many people wanted African Americans and other Americans to be able to mix together freely. They were pleased that Jackie spoke against the laws that did not let him eat at the same restaurants or stay at the same hotels as his white teammates. They admired him for working for equal treatment of African Americans.

Jackie Robinson, center, is mobbed by autograph hunters outside Ebbets Field in Brooklyn, NY.

Jackie Robinson addresses civil rights supporters.

Chapter 4

Life After Baseball

Jackie Robinson retired from baseball in 1956. He was 37 years old. Now, he could spend more time at the family home in Stamford, Connecticut, with Rachel and his children—Sharon, Jackie Jr., and David. There would be no more road trips and night games.

Robinson went to work as a vice president for a chain of restaurants. He continued to work for civil rights. These are the rights of all people to live and work together freely no matter what their religion or skin color. In the civil rights movement, Robinson worked alongside Dr. Martin Luther King Jr.

From left, Floyd Patterson (former heavyweight boxing champ), Ralph Abernathy (civil rights leader and minister), Martin Luther King Jr., and Jackie Robinson at a rally in Birmingham, Alabama.

Robinson also wanted to help poor people. He started a construction company. The company built houses and apartments for people who didn't have much money.

Robinson continued to work against racial segregation in baseball. After he took the first step, many African-American baseball players joined teams in the major leagues. However, Robinson wanted African Americans to be allowed to work as team managers, coaches, and in the league offices as well.

In 1962, Robinson became the first African American elected to baseball's Hall of Fame, a great honor. He was involved with baseball for the rest of his life. Robinson was only 53 years old when he died in 1972.

Robinson believed in the importance of education. Robinson's wife, Rachel, started the Jackie Robinson Foundation a year after his death. The foundation gives money and support to minority youths who need help to get a college education.

In 1960, Jackie Robinson was elected into the Baseball Hall of Fame on the first ballot.

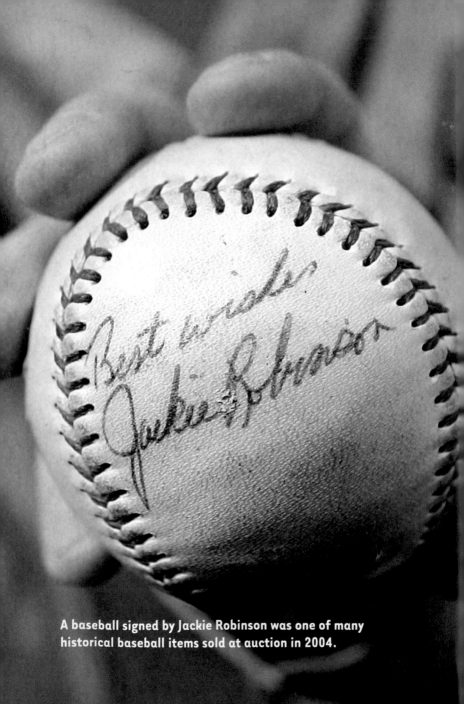

A baseball signed by Jackie Robinson was one of many
historical baseball items sold at auction in 2004.

Chapter 5

Jackie Robinson's Legacy

Robinson's life was a good example to others. He led the way in ending segregation in baseball. By 1959, every major-league baseball team had at least one African-American player. Years later, several baseball teams had hired African Americans as managers.

It is always hard to be the first and set an example. Jackie was the first African American in major-league baseball. Other African-American men and women were also fighting against segregation in other sports and in all areas of life.

Willie O'Ree was the first African American to play professional hockey.

In 1950, Althea Gibson became the first African American to play tennis in the U.S. Nationals. In 1957, Gibson played in the U.S. Nationals again. This time she won the championship.

Willie O'Ree was 14 when he met Jackie Robinson. O'Ree told Robinson he wanted to be a professional hockey player. Robinson reminded him that there were no African Americans playing professional hockey. O'Ree was determined to make his dream come true. In 1958, Willie O'Ree became the first African American to play in the National Hockey League. He played for the Boston Bruins.

Jackie Robinson once said that "a life is not important except in the impact it has on other lives." By speaking out against injustice and fighting for equal rights, Robinson greatly impacted the lives of many. He helped spark the civil rights movement. He opened the door for minorities on and off the baseball field. In 1982, ten years after Jackie Robinson's death, President Reagan awarded him the Presidential Medal of Freedom. This is one of the highest civilian honors an American citizen can receive.

On April 15, 2007, players from the Chicago Cubs and the Cincinnati Reds wore number 42, Robinson's number. That day was the 60th anniversary of his first major-league game.

How to Write an A+ Report

1. Choose a topic.
- Find something that interests you.
- Make sure it is not too big or too small.

2. Find sources.
- Ask your librarian for help.
- Use many different sources: books, magazine articles, and Web sites.

3. Gather information.
- Take notes. Write down the big ideas and interesting details.
- Use your own words.

4. Organize information.
- Sort your notes into groups that make sense.

- Make an outline. Put your groups of notes in the order you want to write your report.

5. Write your report.

- Write an introduction that tells what the report is about.

- Use your outline and notes as you write to make sure you say everything you want to say in the order you want to say it.

- Write an ending that tells about your report.

- Write a title.

6. Revise and edit your report.

- Read your report to make sure it makes sense.

- Read it again to check spelling, punctuation, and grammar.

7. Hand in your report!

Glossary

civil rights	the rights of the people living in a country to freedom and equal treatment under the law
impact	the effect of one person on another
legacy	anything that people hand down to the next generation
officer	a person who leads other people in an organization such as the army
professional	doing something for payment or as a full-time job
segregated	groups of people separated from each other for reasons such as a difference in skin color or religion
self-respect	a sense of your own value as a person
World Series	baseball competition between the winning teams from the National League and the American League

Further Reading

• Books •

Editors of TIME for Kids. *Time for Kids: Jackie Robinson: Strong Inside and Out.* New York: HarperCollins, 2005. Grades 2–4, 48 pages.

Rappoport, Ken. *Profiles in Sports Courage.* Atlanta, GA: Peachtree Publishers, 2006. Grades 5–8, 152 pages.

Robinson, Sharon. *Promises to Keep: How Jackie Robinson Changed America.* New York: Scholastic, 1994. Grades 3–6, 64 pages.

Scott, Richard. *Jackie Robinson* (Black American Series). Los Angeles, CA: Holloway House Publishing Company, 1990. Grade 5 & up, 180 pages.

Supples, Kevin. *Speaking Out: The Civil Rights Movement 1950-1964.* Washington, D.C.: National Geographic Society, 2005. Grades 5–8, 40 pages.

• Web Sites •

Baseball Hall of Fame
www.baseballhalloffame.org

Jackie Robinson Foundation
http://www.jackierobinson.org

Jackie Robinson Site
http://www.jackierobinson.com

Library of Congress American Memory
http://memory.loc.gov/ammem/collections/robinson

National Archives
http://www.archives.gov/education/lessons/jackie-robinson

Index